Taxcafe.co.uk Tax Guides

Dividend Tax Planning

How to Prepare for the 2016/17
Tax Increase

By Carl Bayley BSc ACA
and
Nick Braun PhD

Important Legal Notices:

Taxcafe®
Tax Guide - "Dividend Tax Planning"

Published by:
Taxcafe UK Limited
67 Milton Road
Kirkcaldy KY1 1TL
Tel: (0044) 01592 560081
Email: team@taxcafe.co.uk

First edition, September 2015

ISBN 978-1-907302-99-2

Trademarks
Taxcafe® is a registered trademark of Taxcafe UK Limited. All other logos, trademarks, names and logos in this tax guide may be trademarks of their respective owners.

Disclaimer
Before reading or relying on the content of this tax guide please read the disclaimer carefully.

Pay Less Tax!

...with help from Taxcafe's unique tax guides

All products available online at

www.taxcafe.co.uk

Popular Taxcafe titles include:

- *How to Save Property Tax*
- *Using a Property Company to Save Tax*
- *Tax-Free Capital Gains*
- *Salary versus Dividends*
- *Using a Company to Save Tax*
- *Small Business Tax Saving Tactics*
- *Keeping it Simple: Small Business Bookkeeping, Tax & VAT*
- *Non-Resident & Offshore Tax Planning*
- *How to Save Inheritance Tax*
- *Tax Saving Tactics for Salary Earners*
- *Pension Magic*
- *Isle of Man Tax Saving Guide*
- *How to Save Tax*

Disclaimer

1. This guide is intended as **general guidance** only and does NOT constitute accountancy, tax, investment or other professional advice.

2. The authors and Taxcafe UK Limited make no representations or warranties with respect to the accuracy or completeness of this publication and cannot accept any responsibility or liability for any loss or risk, personal or otherwise, which may arise, directly or indirectly, from reliance on information contained in this publication.

3. Please note that tax legislation, the law and practices of Government and regulatory authorities (e.g. HM Revenue & Customs) are constantly changing. We therefore recommend that for accountancy, tax, investment or other professional advice, you consult a suitably qualified accountant, tax advisor, financial adviser, or other professional adviser.

4. Please also note that your personal circumstances may vary from the general examples provided in this guide and your professional adviser will be able to provide specific advice based on your personal circumstances.

5. This guide covers UK taxation only and any references to 'tax' or 'taxation', unless the contrary is expressly stated, refer to UK taxation only. Please note that references to the 'UK' do not include the Channel Islands or the Isle of Man. Foreign tax implications are beyond the scope of this guide.

6. All persons described in the examples in this guide are entirely fictional. Any similarities to actual persons, living or dead, or to fictional characters created by any other author, are entirely coincidental.

About the Authors & Taxcafe

Carl Bayley is the author of a series of Taxcafe guides designed specifically for the layman. Carl's particular speciality is his ability to take the weird, complex and inexplicable world of taxation and set it out in the kind of clear, straightforward language that taxpayers themselves can understand. As he often says himself, "my job is to translate 'tax' into English".

In addition to being a recognised author, Carl has often spoken on taxation on radio and television, including the BBC's *It's Your Money* programme and the Jeremy Vine Show on Radio 2.

A chartered accountant by training, Carl is currently Chairman of the Tax Faculty of the Institute of Chartered Accountants in England and Wales and is also a member of the Institute's governing Council.

Nick Braun founded Taxcafe.co.uk in 1999, along with his partner, Aileen Smith. As the driving force behind the company, their aim is to provide affordable plain-English tax information for private individuals and investors, business owners, IFAs and accountants.

Since then Taxcafe has become one of the best-known tax publishers in the UK and has won several business awards.

Nick has been involved in the tax publishing world since 1989 as a writer, editor and publisher. He holds a doctorate in economics from the University of Glasgow, where he was awarded the prestigious William Glen Scholarship and later became a Research Fellow. Prior to that, he graduated with distinction from the University of South Africa, the country's oldest university, earning the highest results in economics in the university's history.

Contents

Introduction

In the July 2015 Budget it was announced that the tax treatment of dividends will be completely changed at the start of the 2016/17 tax year on 6 April 2016.

Dividend tax credits will be abolished, so it will no longer be necessary to gross up your dividends to calculate your tax. All tax calculations will work with the amount of dividend actually paid.

For ease of illustration, we will generally refer to the amount of dividend actually paid, or deemed to be paid, as the 'cash' dividend. This does not necessarily mean that it is literally paid in cash, as dividends are sometimes effectively paid by way of accounting entries, or by some other means.

Nonetheless, however your dividends are paid, the abolition of the tax credit will make your tax calculations a lot simpler.

That's the good news. The bad news is that new tax rates for 'cash' dividends have been announced that are 7.5% higher than the existing rates. The first £5,000 of dividend income will, however, be tax free thanks to a new "dividend allowance".

This guide explains how dividends will be taxed next year and what action you should take *this year* to reduce your tax. In particular, we examine whether company owners should pay themselves a bigger dividend this year before the tax rates go up and how much tax you are likely to save.

Chapters 1 and 2 briefly cover some tax basics, including the importance of taking a small tax-free salary and the key income tax thresholds where higher tax rates apply – there's no point paying yourself a bigger dividend this year if it will be taxed more heavily this year than next year!

Company owners can only pay themselves dividends if their companies have sufficient distributable profits. Chapter 3 explains what this means in practice.

Chapters 4 and 5 explain how dividends are currently taxed, how they will be taxed next year, and exactly how much extra tax you are likely to pay.

Chapters 6 and 7 cover other recent and potential tax changes facing company owners. There may be more bad news on the horizon but there were some welcome announcements in the July 2015 Budget, including an increase in the national insurance employment allowance and further cuts to corporation tax.

Saving Tax!

The remaining chapters cover tax planning issues.

Chapter 8 shows you how to calculate the maximum tax-free dividend you can extract from your company this year. This is the last big tax-free dividend allowance you'll get so it's important not to waste it!

Once you've taken the maximum tax-free dividend, Chapter 9 examines whether you should pay yourself an even bigger dividend this year, even though 25% tax (or more) will be payable.

Chapter 10 shows how company owners who are normally higher-rate taxpayers can save tax by paying themselves a bigger dividend this year and smaller dividend next year. In the example in this chapter the company owner saves £2,400 tax by doing exactly that.

If you want to pay yourself a bigger dividend this year Chapter 11 shows you how to avoid the £50,000-£60,000 tax bracket where the child benefit charge applies and dividends are taxed at extortionate rates.

If your taxable income is normally over £60,000 (i.e. you effectively lose all your child benefit) one thing you may be able to do is pay yourself a bigger dividend this year and smaller dividend next year so that you avoid the child benefit charge next year and have less dividend income taxed at the new 32.5% higher rate. In Chapter 11 we will see how one taxpayer saves £3,626 by following this strategy.

Chapter 12 looks at some of the issues facing high income earners (those earning over £100,000 or £150,000).

Chapter 13 shows how company owners can split their dividend income with their spouses to save tax and why this strategy is likely to continue to be popular.

Finally, Chapter 14 looks at how the dividend tax changes will affect company owners' pension contribution decisions, e.g. whether you or the company should make the pension contributions.

Scope of this Guide & Limitations

At present details of the new dividend tax regime are fairly sketchy – all we have is the initial Budget announcement plus a factsheet issued by HMRC.

It is possible therefore that further details will emerge or other tax changes will be announced that alter some of the information in this guide.

Although the guide covers a fair amount of ground, it does not cover every possible scenario – that would be impossible without making it much longer and possibly much more difficult to digest.

Companies come in many different shapes and sizes, as do their owners, so it is possible that the information contained in this guide will not be relevant to your circumstances.

The main focus of this tax guide is *income tax* planning: helping company owners pay less tax on their dividends. Steps that you take to reduce one type of tax can have an adverse impact on your liability to pay other taxes.

There are also *non-tax* factors that have to be considered when deciding how much money you withdraw from your company and in what form. In some instances other considerations will outweigh any potential tax savings.

For all of these reasons it is vital that you obtain professional advice before taking any action based on information contained in this guide. The authors and Taxcafe UK Ltd cannot accept any responsibility for any loss which may arise as a consequence of any action taken, or any decision to refrain from taking action, as a result of reading this guide

Chapter 1

Tax-Free Salaries

One of the advantages of being a company owner is you can often decide whether any distribution of the company's money is classified as salary or dividend.

Although *dividends* are the focus of this guide – in particular the increase in dividend tax rates coming on 6 April 2016 – it's important to point out that the first thing almost every company owner should do is pay themselves a small salary.

A small salary is usually more tax efficient than a dividend because it is both tax free in the hands of the director and provides a corporation tax saving for the company as well (because it's a tax deductible expense).

Dividends, on the other hand, are paid out of a company's *after-tax profits*, i.e., after corporation tax has already been paid.

Because small salaries are so tax efficient you should also consider paying them to your spouse/partner and children (including minor children) wherever possible.

How Much Salary?

There are three important income tax and national insurance thresholds for the current 2015/16 tax year:

- Employee's national insurance   £8,060
- Employer's national insurance   £8,112
- Income tax   £10,600

The most tax efficient level of salary depends on a variety of factors, including how much income you have from other sources, the total level of your income and whether your company has any spare national insurance employment allowance (which provides most companies with a £2,000 national insurance saving; increasing to £3,000 in 2016/17).

To keep things simple for now we'll assume that the director does not have any income from other sources.

Where the company does NOT have to pay any national insurance on the directors' own salaries (i.e. where the national insurance employment allowance is not used up paying salaries to other employees) a salary of £10,600 will generally be most tax efficient.

Where the company DOES have to pay national insurance on the directors' salaries, the most tax efficient level of salary is either £8,060 or £8,112.

A salary of £8,060 is completely tax free: there is no national insurance or income tax. A salary of £8,112 attracts a small amount of employee's national insurance but is actually a tiny bit more tax efficient because the additional corporation tax relief outweighs the national insurance cost.

However, the extra tax saving is tiny (a few pounds) so in many of the examples in this guide we will assume for simplicity that the director takes a completely tax-free salary of £8,060 (and in some examples we'll use £8,000 because it's a nice round number!).

Income from Other Sources

If you do have taxable income from other sources (e.g. rental property), you may be able to enjoy a small increase in your after-tax income by taking a smaller salary.

How is your optimal salary calculated? Generally speaking, by deducting your other income from your income tax personal allowance. For example, if you have taxable rental income of £4,000 in 2015/16, your optimal salary would be:

$$£10,600 - £4,000 = £6,600$$

However, increasing this up to £8,060 is generally tax neutral (the extra £1,460 creates a 20% tax cost for you, but a 20% saving for your company).

Furthermore, there is one very important reason why you may decide not to reduce your salary too much and that is to protect your state pension (see below).

Income over £100,000

Once your income rises above £100,000 your personal allowance starts to be withdrawn; once your income reaches £121,200 it is completely taken away.

In these circumstances, it may be possible to achieve additional tax savings by paying yourself a smaller salary or no salary at all.

For example, earlier it was stated that where the company does not have to pay any national insurance, a salary of £10,600 will generally be most tax efficient.

However, where the company owner's taxable income exceeds £121,200 (no personal allowance remaining), a tax saving of several hundred pounds can be achieved by taking a salary of £8,060 instead of £10,600. It may be possible to achieve further tax savings by reducing the salary even further.

Where the company does have to pay national insurance and the optimal salary is generally £8,060, a small tax saving can be achieved by taking a smaller salary when the company owner's taxable income exceeds £121,200. However, the tax saving is not very impressive (less than a couple of hundred pounds in most cases, which is a very small saving for someone with so much income).

Once again you may decide to not reduce your salary too much so as to protect your state pension (see below):

State Pension Entitlement

To protect your state pension entitlement you should pay yourself a salary that is greater than the national insurance 'lower earnings limit'.

For 2015/16, the lower earnings limit is £112 per week which requires a total annual salary of at least £5,824.

Thus if you want to protect your state pension entitlement, a salary of at least £5,824 should be paid in 2015/16 in preference to taking dividends.

Bigger Salaries

In practice not all directors take a salary of £8,060 or £10,600 or any other amount that may be "optimal" or "tax efficient". Many will take a bigger salary because, even though a big chunk of national insurance may be payable, a salary is often a simple way to take cash out of the business each month (especially when you're paying other employees anyway). Dividends, on the other hand, can't be paid unless it can be shown that the company has distributable profits (see Chapter 3).

Salaries do have to be justified by the level of work carried out, otherwise the company will be denied corporation tax relief. This isn't an issue for most company owners who work in their businesses but problems could arise if you decide to pay salaries to other members of your family. Salaries also have to be reported to HMRC under the new Real Time Information (RTI) regime. Your accountant can do this for you but you will, of course, incur fees.

Summary

Company owners should always consider paying themselves a small tax-free salary. For those without income from other sources the "optimal" salary levels are £10,600 (where no employer's national insurance is payable) and £8,060 or £8,112 (where employer's national insurance is payable).

Where the company owner does have income from other sources a smaller salary may be more tax efficient, although a salary of at least £5,824 is required to protect your state pension entitlement.

A smaller salary can also be more tax efficient once your income reaches £121,200 and your personal allowance is completely taken away (again, a salary of at least £5,824 is required to protect your state pension entitlement).

If the company owner needs more income than the small "optimal" salary, as most probably will, generally the most tax-efficient route is to take the rest of your income as dividends.

However, that's not the end of the matter. The next thing the company owner has to watch out for is a series of tax thresholds, where higher tax rates kick in.

Chapter 2

The Key Tax Thresholds

One of the advantages of being a company owner is you can often choose between taking a salary or dividend. Another advantage is you can control *how much* income you withdraw in total, which gives you significant control over your personal tax bill.

Unlike sole traders, who pay tax each year on ALL the profits of the business, company owners only pay tax on the money they actually withdraw from their companies.

With dividend tax rates going up on 6 April 2016, many company owners may decide to extract more dividend income this year and less next year.

However, you have to be careful about doing this if your additional dividends will push you into a higher tax bracket this year. In other words, you have to be careful about trying to avoid next year's tax hike by paying even higher tax rates this year.

We'll take a closer look at this issue in the chapters that follow but for now it's worth stating that the key tax thresholds for 2015/16 are as follows:

- £42,385   Higher-rate tax
- £50,000   Child benefit tax charge
- £100,000   Personal allowance withdrawal
- £150,000   Additional rate tax

If your total taxable income is less than £42,385 this year your dividends will be tax free. Your company will be subject to corporation tax on the profits paid out as dividends (typically at 20%) but there will be no further income tax payable by you.

If you withdraw additional dividend income over the higher-rate threshold, you will pay tax at an effective rate of 25% on your additional cash dividends.

What this means is that company owners who *normally* have taxable income below the higher-rate threshold have to be careful about taking additional dividend income this year if this will push them over the higher-rate threshold.

If you have children and child benefit is being claimed the next threshold to watch out for is £50,000. Child benefit is gradually withdrawn when the highest earner in the household has income between £50,000 and £60,000. This is done through the high income child benefit charge which is collected when you submit your tax return.

The child benefit charge creates higher effective marginal tax rates on dividend income in the £50,000-£60,000 tax bracket. These start at 37% for parents with one qualifying child, rising to 61% for those with four children, and even higher for those with larger families.

Thus company owners who normally have taxable income below £50,000 have to be careful about taking additional dividend income this year if this will push them over the £50,000 threshold.

The next important tax threshold is £100,000. Once your taxable income rises above £100,000, your personal allowance is gradually withdrawn. Once your income reaches £121,200 you will have no personal allowance left at all.

Company owners with income in the £100,000 to £121,200 bracket face paying income tax at an effective rate of up to 48.6% on any additional cash dividends they withdraw.

Thus company owners who normally have taxable income below £100,000 have to be careful about taking additional dividend income this year if it will take them over the £100,000 threshold.

Once your income rises above £150,000 you become an additional-rate taxpayer. The effective income tax rate on dividend income then rises from 25% to 30.6%.

Thus company owners who normally have taxable income below £150,000 have to be careful about taking additional dividend income this year if it will take them over the £150,000 threshold.

Summary

With dividend tax rates going up on 6 April 2016, many company owners may decide to extract more dividend income this year and perhaps less next year.

However, you have to watch out for the key tax thresholds where higher tax rates apply.

Furthermore, as we shall see in Chapter 4, the tax thresholds for 2015/16 apply to your *gross* dividend income, not the actual cash you extract from your company.

Thus, if you are not careful, you could end up taking too much income out of your company and going over one of the thresholds.

Before we take a closer look at how dividends are grossed up and taxed it's important to address one other important issue when it comes to paying yourself dividend income: the availability of distributable profits.

Chapter 3

Dividends and Distributable Profits

Under Company Law, a company cannot pay a dividend unless it has sufficient distributable profits to cover it. A company's distributable profits are its accumulated realised profits, less accumulated realised losses.

This information can generally be found in the most recent annual accounts. However, it's probably wise to speak to your accountant before paying any dividends to make sure the company does indeed have sufficient distributable profits.

Example
Tony owns Fast Tony Ltd, a manufacturer of ready meals and snacks. He is the company's only shareholder. The company's accounting period runs from 1 January to 31 December. In June 2015 Tony signs off the company's 2014 accounts which cover the period 1 January to 31 December 2014.

In the "Notes to the Financial Statements" he finds the following information in the section entitled "Reserves":

	Profit and Loss Account
	£
At 1 January 2014	40,000
Profit for the year	20,000
Dividends	(45,000)
At 31 December 2014	15,000

At the start of 2014 the company had reserves of £40,000. We then add the £20,000 (after-tax) profit made in 2014 and subtract the £45,000 dividend Tony paid himself at some point in 2014. Thus the company had reserves of £15,000 at the end of the year on 31 December 2014.

Armed with this information, Tony can pay himself a cash dividend of up to £15,000 (providing he hasn't paid himself any dividends so far in 2015 and providing the company has not realised losses since 31 December 2014).

What if Tony wants to pay himself a bigger dividend before dividend tax rates increase on 6 April 2016?

Even though Tony may have strong reasons to believe that the company has been making profits since December 2014, an additional dividend cannot be paid unless more up-to-date accounts are prepared which prove that there are sufficient distributable profits.

Fast Tony Ltd's current accounting period runs from 1 January 2015 to 31 December 2015, so Tony can probably afford to wait until the end of the year before doing anything. He can then ask his accountant to push out the company's accounts (which will show the current level of distributable profits) and pay himself an additional dividend before 6 April 2016.

Example continued
In February 2016 Tony signs off the company's 2015 accounts which cover the period 1 January to 31 December 2015. The company's profit and loss account is as follows:

	Profit and Loss Account
	£
At 1 January 2015	15,000
Profit for the year	40,000
Dividends	(15,000)
At 31 December 2015	40,000

Tony can pay himself an additional dividend of up to £40,000. He decides to take just £15,892 because he calculates that, coupled with his existing dividend of £15,000 and small company salary of £8,060, this is the maximum amount of tax-free dividend income he can withdraw in 2015/16 (see Chapter 8).

Interim Accounts

If your company does not have sufficient distributable profits to pay dividends and its current accounting period ends close to or after 5 April 2016, it may be necessary to prepare interim accounts. In these circumstances the potential tax savings will have to be weighed against any additional accountancy fees.

Bigger Profits = Bigger Dividends

In some cases, where dividends are to be paid out of an accounting period which is still running, it may be desirable to postpone any discretionary business expenditure (e.g. advertising) to a later accounting period.

The idea here is to increase the company's profits: less spending means bigger profits which means bigger dividends can be paid.

The downside, of course, is that postponing business expenditure will usually lead to an increase in the company's corporation tax bill. However, if the expenditure is merely postponed, and not cancelled, then there will be a corresponding decrease in the next period's corporation tax charge, so there is no overall loss: whereas the savings arising by being able to take higher dividends in the current tax year may be permanent.

Alternatively, a good way to keep accounting profits high (to enable higher dividends to be taken), but still keep the company's taxable profits low, is to replace discretionary expenditure on items such as advertising with expenditure on equipment and other assets qualifying for capital allowances instead.

In most cases, expenditure on qualifying business assets (except cars) will attract immediate tax relief at 100% thanks to the annual investment allowance. (Some care needs to be taken, as there are limits to the amount of allowance available, although these are generally pretty generous in the context of a small owner-managed company)

Whilst this expenditure will often attract 100% tax relief, the reduction in the company's accounting profits will usually be much less. This will depend on the company's own accounting policies. Typically, however, expenditure on new equipment will only reduce accounting profits for the same period by around 10% to 25% of that expenditure. With 20% tax relief on the full amount expended, the profits after tax available to fund a dividend might even go up!

Bigger Dividends & Cashflow

If you prefer to retain the cash in your company, it may be possible for a dividend to be declared but not paid out. The dividend can simply be credited to the director's loan account and withdrawn at a later date when it is more convenient.

HMRC generally accepts this approach where the cash is available but the director chooses not to extract that cash from the company. Difficulties may arise where this approach is used in a situation where there is no cash available to fund the dividend, although the legal basis for this view is uncertain.

Note that the director will still be subject to income tax on any dividend that has been declared but not paid out (although basic-rate taxpayers do not pay any tax on their dividends this year). In practice, this means that, where the company owner is a higher-rate taxpayer, it may be necessary to pay a portion of the dividend in cash to help the director pay their tax bill.

Dividend Formalities & Paperwork

It is essential to ensure that dividends are properly declared and you have the supporting paperwork to prove it.

This includes:

- Holding a directors' board meeting to recommend the dividend payment (with printed minutes to prove the meeting took place)

- Holding a general meeting of the company's members (i.e. shareholders) to approve the dividend payment (with printed minutes to prove the meeting took place)

- Issuing a dividend voucher to each shareholder

See the Appendix for sample documentation.

Chapter 4

Dividend Tax Basics 2015/16

The income tax rates applying to dividends are lower than those for salaries and most other types of income because dividends are paid out of a company's *after-tax* profits, i.e. money that has already been taxed in the company's hands.

The effective income tax rates applying to *cash dividends* in 2015/16 are:

- Basic-rate taxpayers 0%
- Higher-rate taxpayers 25%
- Additional rate taxpayers 30.6%

As explained in the introduction, 'cash dividends' means the actual payment from the company to the director/shareholder.

Gross Dividends vs Cash Dividends

For the current 2015/16 tax year most taxpayers receive a personal allowance of £10,600 and basic-rate band of £31,785 which means you become a higher-rate taxpayer when your income exceeds £42,385. When your income exceeds £100,000 your personal allowance is gradually withdrawn and if your income exceeds £150,000 you become an additional-rate taxpayer.

However, those thresholds are for *gross* dividends, not the actual *cash* dividends you receive from your company. Whereas company owners are mostly interested in their cash dividends, most tax calculations work with gross dividends.

If you want to minimise the income tax payable on your dividend income it is essential to understand the difference between gross dividends and cash dividends.

Gross dividends are found by dividing cash dividends by 0.9:

Gross dividends = Cash dividends/0.9

For example, if you pay yourself a cash dividend of £90, the gross dividend is £100 (£90/0.9). The £10 difference is what's known as the dividend tax credit.

Gross dividends are taxed at the following rates:

- Basic-rate taxpayers   10%
- Higher-rate taxpayers   32.5%
- Additional rate taxpayers   37.5%

However, to calculate your final income tax bill you subtract the 10% dividend tax credit. The *effective* income tax rates on gross dividends are thus:

- Basic-rate taxpayers   0%
- Higher-rate taxpayers   22.5%
- Additional rate taxpayers   27.5%

It's all unnecessarily complicated – a bit like climbing over a mountain instead of walking around the side. However, from next year onwards dividend tax calculations will become a lot simpler (see Chapter 5).

Example – Basic-Rate Taxpayer

Stuart is a company owner with a salary of £8,060 and cash dividend of £20,000 (£22,222 gross dividend). His total taxable income is thus £30,282.

His salary is tax-free because it is covered by his income tax personal allowance.

The income tax on his dividends can be calculated quickly by remembering that basic-rate taxpayers effectively pay 0% tax on their dividends. With a total income of £30,282 Stuart falls below the £42,385 higher-rate threshold and is a basic-rate taxpayer. There is no tax payable on his dividends.

Example – Higher-Rate Taxpayer

Robert is a company owner with a salary of £8,060 and cash dividend of £35,000 (£38,889 gross dividend). His total taxable income is thus £46,949.

His salary is tax-free because it is covered by his income tax personal allowance.

The income tax on his dividends can be calculated quickly by remembering that higher-rate taxpayers effectively pay 22.5% tax on gross dividends that exceed the £42,385 higher-rate threshold (dividends that fall within the basic-rate band are effectively tax-free).

The amount of his income subject to higher-rate tax is:

$$£46,949 - £42,385 = £4,564$$

His total income tax bill is therefore £1,027:

$$£4,564 \times 22.5\% = £1,027$$

Example – Personal Allowance Withdrawal

Alpesh is a company owner with a salary of £8,060* and cash dividend of £100,000 (£111,111 gross dividend). His total taxable income is thus £119,171. Because his income exceeds £100,000 his personal allowance is reduced from £10,600 to £1,014.

This means 20% tax is payable on £7,046 of his salary, producing a tax bill of £1,409. His basic-rate band available for tax-free dividends is also reduced from £31,785 to £24,739.

The remaining £86,372 of his gross dividend income is taxed at an effective rate of 22.5%, producing a tax bill of £19,434.

His total tax bill is therefore £20,843.

* As we saw in Chapter 1, £8,060 is not necessarily the "optimal" salary for Alpesh. Nevertheless we'll assume this is the salary he takes to keep the example simple.

Example – Additional-Rate Taxpayer

Maeve is a company owner with a salary of £8,060 and cash dividend of £200,000 (£222,222 gross dividend). Her total taxable income is thus £230,282. Because her income exceeds £150,000 she is an additional-rate taxpayer.

Her income tax personal allowance is also completely withdrawn. This means she will pay 20% income tax on her salary – £1,612 – and her basic-rate band available for tax-free dividends will be reduced from £31,785 to £23,725 (£31,785 less £8,060 used up by her salary).

The next £118,215 of her gross dividend income (£150,000 less £31,785) is subject to higher-rate tax at an effective rate of 22.5%, resulting in additional tax of £26,598. The remaining £80,282 of gross dividend income takes her over the £150,000 threshold and is taxed at an effective rate of 27.5%, resulting in additional tax of £22,078.

Her total tax bill is thus £50,288.

(Again, £8,060 is not necessarily the "optimal" salary for Maeve but for simplicity we'll assume this is the salary she takes.)

Confusing Gross Dividends and Cash Dividends

If you want to ensure that your dividend income in 2015/16 does not breach the £42,385, £100,000 or £150,000 thresholds it is critical to remember that it is the *gross dividend* that is relevant, not the cash dividend actually received.

Example

Matthew is a company owner who has not extracted any dividend income from his company so far in 2015/16. He has no other taxable income. He decides to pay himself a cash dividend of £42,000, under the mistaken belief that he will pay 0% tax because his income is below the higher-rate threshold (£42,385 in 2015/16).

However, Matthew's gross dividend income is actually £46,667 and his income tax bill is £963:

£42,000/0.9 = £46,667 - £42,385 = £4,282 x 22.5% = £963

Chapter 5

Dividend Tax Basics 2016/17

In the July 2015 Budget it was announced that the taxation of dividends will be completely changed at the start of the 2016/17 tax year on 6 April 2016.

Dividend tax credits will be abolished, so it will no longer be necessary to gross up your cash dividends to calculate your tax. All tax calculations will work with cash dividends only and will therefore be a lot simpler.

That's the good news. The bad news is that new tax rates for cash dividends have been announced that are 7.5% higher than the existing effective rates.

The first £5,000 of dividend income will, however, be tax free thanks to a new "dividend allowance". All taxpayers, regardless of income, will be able to benefit from the £5,000 dividend allowance.

For those receiving dividends in excess of the new £5,000 allowance, the following income tax rates will apply (the current effective rates on cash dividends received in 2015/16 are included for comparison):

	2015/16	**2016/17**
Basic-rate taxpayers	0%	7.5%
Higher-rate taxpayers	25%	32.5%
Additional-rate taxpayers	30.6%	38.1%

This change has been designed to extract more tax from company owners who take most of their income as dividends.

Many company owners may therefore be thinking about taking bigger than normal dividends before the current 2015/16 tax year ends on 5 April 2016.

However, before we explore this subject in detail it's important to explain in more detail how dividends will be taxed from next year onwards.

2016/17 Tax Thresholds

For the 2016/17 tax year, starting on 6 April 2016, the key income tax numbers for most taxpayers will be as follows:

- £11,000   Personal allowance
- £32,000   Basic-rate band
- £43,000   Higher-rate threshold

Just like this year, once your income rises above £50,000 you may be subject to the high income child benefit charge; once your income rises above £100,000 you will start to lose your personal allowance and once your income exceeds £150,000 you will become an additional-rate taxpayer.

Cash Dividends = Lower Taxable Income

Dividend tax rates are going up but the thresholds where they kick in are going up too. This is because your dividends will no longer be grossed up, artificially pushing you into a higher tax bracket.

In other words, in future you will be able to extract more dividend income from your company before you become a higher-rate taxpayer and before you lose your child benefit or personal allowance or become an additional-rate taxpayer.

For example, this year a company owner with no other income can withdraw a cash dividend of £38,147 before becoming a higher-rate taxpayer and paying 25% tax.

Next year (in 2016/17) it will be possible to withdraw a cash dividend of up to £43,000 before becoming a higher-rate taxpayer and paying 32.5% tax.

Don't be mistaken, almost every company owner will pay more tax under the new regime but for some the pain will be reduced by having more income falling into a lower tax bracket.

The New Dividend Allowance

The £5,000 dividend allowance is not as generous as we first hoped. Company owners will NOT enjoy an additional standalone amount of £5,000 tax free. Instead the dividend allowance will typically use up some of your basic-rate band.

For example, if you have a £50,000 dividend and no other income, the first £11,000 will be tax free thanks to your personal allowance and the next £5,000 will be tax free thanks to the dividend allowance. However, only £27,000 of your remaining income will be taxed at 7.5% because the £5,000 dividend allowance will count as part of your £32,000 basic-rate band. The final £7,000 will then be taxed at 32.5%.

The dividend allowance only uses up your basic-rate band if, like many directors, you have dividend income subject to basic-rate tax. As we shall see later, it works differently if you have a lot of other income and all your dividends are subject to higher-rate tax.

The New Dividend Tax Regime – Examples

Let's take a look at some sample 2016/17 calculations using the same company owners we met in Chapter 4 and see how their tax bills change. To keep things simple we'll assume once again they all take a salary of £8,060, even though this is not necessarily the "optimal" amount. We use £8,060 because the national insurance thresholds for 2016/17 have not been announced yet and because it makes it easier to compare the 2015/16 and 2016/17 tax bills.

Example – Basic-Rate Taxpayer

Stuart is a company owner with a salary of £8,060 and cash dividend of £20,000. His total income is thus £28,060.

His salary is tax-free because it is covered by his personal allowance. The first £2,940 of his dividend income is tax free, being covered by the remainder of his personal allowance (£11,000 - £8,060). The next £5,000 of his dividend income is also tax-free thanks to the new dividend allowance. The final £12,060 of his dividend income is taxed at 7.5%, producing a total tax bill of £905.

Stuart's tax bill goes up from £0 in 2015/16 to £905 in 2016/17.

Example – Higher-Rate Taxpayer

Robert is a company owner with a salary of £8,060 and cash dividend of £35,000. His total income is thus £43,060.

His salary is tax-free as it is covered by his personal allowance and the first £2,940 of his dividend income is tax free, being covered by the remainder of his personal allowance (£11,000 - £8,060).

The next £5,000 of his dividend income is also tax-free thanks to the new dividend allowance. The dividend allowance uses up £5,000 of his £32,000 basic-rate band so just £27,000 of his dividend income is taxed at 7.5%, producing a tax bill of £2,025. The final £60 of his dividend income takes him over the higher-rate threshold and is taxed at 32.5%, producing a tax bill of £20.

Robert's tax bill goes up from £1,027 in 2015/16 to £2,045 in 2016/17 – an increase of £1,018.

Example – Personal Allowance Withdrawal

Alpesh is a company owner with a salary of £8,060 and cash dividend of £100,000. His total taxable income is thus £108,060. His personal allowance is reduced from £11,000 to £6,970. Thus £1,090 of his salary is taxed at 20% (£8,060 - £6,970), producing a tax bill of £218.

The first £5,000 of his dividend income is tax free, being covered by the new dividend allowance.

The next £25,910 of his dividend income is covered by his remaining basic-rate band (£32,000 - £1,090 - £5,000) and taxed at 7.5%, producing a tax bill of £1,943.

The remaining £69,090 of his dividend income is taxed at 32.5%, producing a tax bill of £22,454.

His total tax bill is therefore £24,615.

Alpesh's tax bill goes up from £20,843 in 2015/16 to £24,615 in 2016/17, an increase of £3,772.

Example – Additional-Rate Taxpayer

Maeve is a company owner with a salary of £8,060 and dividend of £200,000. Her total income is thus £208,060. Because her income exceeds £150,000 she is an additional-rate taxpayer.

The first £5,000 of her dividend income is tax free but her income tax personal allowance is completely withdrawn. This means she will pay 20% income tax on her salary – £1,612 – and her remaining basic-rate band will be reduced to just £18,940 (£32,000 - £8,060 salary - £5,000 dividend allowance). She will thus pay 7.5% tax on £18,940 of her dividend income (£1,420).

The next £118,000 of her dividend (£150,000 less £32,000) is subject to higher-rate tax at 32.5%, resulting in additional tax of £38,350. The remaining £58,060 of dividend income takes her over the £150,000 threshold and is taxed at 38.1%, resulting in additional tax of £22,121.

Maeve's tax bill goes up from £50,288 in 2015/16 to £63,503 in 2016/17 – an increase of £13,215.

Table 1 shows you how much extra tax you could end up paying if you extract the same amount of income from your company in both 2015/16 and 2016/17.

To keep things simple we've assumed that a salary of £8,060 is taken in both tax years (see Chapter 1). Although many company owners will pay themselves a different amount of salary, the table gives you a flavour of how the increase in dividend tax rates will affect taxpayers with different amounts of income.

For example, someone who takes a salary of £8,060 and cash dividend of £50,000 this year and in 2016/17 will pay £2,143 more tax in 2016/17.

TABLE 1
Income Tax 2015/16 versus 2016/17

Salary	Cash Dividend	Total Income	Tax 2015/16	Tax 2016/17	Increase
8,060	5,000	13,060	0	0	0
8,060	10,000	18,060	0	155	155
8,060	15,000	23,060	0	530	530
8,060	20,000	28,060	0	905	905
8,060	25,000	33,060	0	1,280	1,280
8,060	30,000	38,060	0	1,655	1,655
8,060	35,000	43,060	1,027	2,045	1,018
8,060	40,000	48,060	2,277	3,670	1,393
8,060	45,000	53,060	3,527	5,295	1,768
8,060	50,000	58,060	4,777	6,920	2,143
8,060	55,000	63,060	6,027	8,545	2,518
8,060	60,000	68,060	7,277	10,170	2,893
8,060	65,000	73,060	8,527	11,795	3,268
8,060	70,000	78,060	9,777	13,420	3,643
8,060	75,000	83,060	11,027	15,045	4,018
8,060	80,000	88,060	12,277	16,670	4,393
8,060	85,000	93,060	13,809	18,295	4,486
8,060	90,000	98,060	15,982	19,920	3,938
8,060	95,000	103,060	18,412	22,042	3,630
8,060	100,000	108,060	20,843	24,615	3,772
8,060	105,000	113,060	22,524	27,366	4,842
8,060	110,000	118,060	23,774	30,116	6,342
8,060	115,000	123,060	25,024	32,627	7,603
8,060	120,000	128,060	26,274	34,252	7,978
8,060	125,000	133,060	27,524	35,877	8,353
8,060	130,000	138,060	28,899	37,502	8,603
8,060	135,000	143,060	30,427	39,127	8,700
8,060	140,000	148,060	31,955	40,752	8,797
8,060	145,000	153,060	33,482	42,548	9,066
8,060	150,000	158,060	35,010	44,453	9,443

Of course, the increase in tax is doubled up where the company is owned equally by a couple. For example, a couple who both receive a salary of £8,060 and dividend of £30,000 will pay £3,310 more tax in 2016/17.

And of course, as things stand, the increase in dividend tax rates is permanent. So if you end up paying £1,000 more tax next year you could end up paying £1,000 more tax each year from now on (although there are likely to be other tax changes for better or worse in the years ahead – see Chapters 6 and 7).

One of the messages from Table 1 is that the dividend tax increase is not entirely fair. For example, someone who takes a dividend of £30,000 will see their tax bill rise by £1,655 but someone who takes a dividend of £40,000 will see their tax bill rise by just £1,393.

Someone who takes a dividend of £75,000 will see their tax bill rise by £4,018 but someone who takes a dividend of £100,000 will see their tax bill rise by just £3,772.

It all comes down to the fact that dividends will no longer be grossed up, so some taxpayers will end up with more income in a lower tax bracket next year.

However, whether the new dividend tax regime is "fair" or not is largely irrelevant to the average company owner. A far more important question is: "What can I do about it?", or more specifically: "Should I pay myself a bigger dividend in 2015/16?"

This is the question we will answer in the chapters ahead.

However, before we do that it's important to explain how the new dividend allowance operates when you have lots of non-dividend income, for example a big salary or a significant amount of rental income.

Taxpayers with Lots of Non-Dividend Income

The dividend allowance only forms part of your basic-rate band if you have dividend income that falls into the basic-rate band. It works differently if your basic-rate band is completely used up by other income, e.g. salary or rental income.

The way to think about it is like this: dividends are always treated as the top slice of your income and taxed at your highest marginal rate. The dividend allowance exempts the bottom £5,000 of that income from tax. So if you have dividend income taxed at both 7.5% and 32.5%, the dividend allowance will exempt some of the income taxed at 7.5%.

But if ALL of your dividend income is taxed at 32.5% (because you have lots of other income, e.g. rental income) the dividend allowance will be part of your higher-rate band and you'll pay 0% tax instead of 32.5% tax on £5,000 of your dividend income.

Example
In 2016/17 Brendan has a £40,000 salary and £10,000 dividend. The first £11,000 of his salary is covered by his personal allowance and the next £29,000 falls into the basic-rate band where it's taxed at 20%; leaving him with £3,000 of basic-rate band available. £5,000 of his dividend income is tax free, thanks to the new dividend allowance. The first £3,000 uses up the remainder of his basic-rate band, leaving £2,000 of dividend allowance to use in the higher-rate band. The remaining £5,000 of his dividend income is taxed at the 32.5% higher rate.

Example
In 2016/17 Julia has a £43,000 salary and £30,000 dividend. Her salary uses up her personal allowance and basic-rate band and takes her up to the higher-rate threshold. The first £5,000 of her dividend income is covered by the dividend allowance, leaving £25,000 subject to tax at the 32.5% higher rate.

The dividend allowance does not form part of her basic-rate band because none of her dividend income falls into the basic-rate band.

Example

In 2016/17 Leon has a £130,000 salary and £50,000 dividend. With this much income his personal allowance is completely withdrawn.

The first £5,000 of his dividend income is covered by the new dividend allowance, leaving £15,000 taxed at the 32.5% higher rate. Along with his salary this takes Leon up to the £150,000 additional-rate threshold. The final £30,000 of his dividend income is taxed at 38.1%.

Note, Leon has dividend income taxed at both the higher rate and additional rate. The dividend allowance reduces the amount of his dividend income taxed at the 32.5% higher rate.

Example

In 2016/17 Martin has a £100,000 salary, £50,000 of rental income and £50,000 dividend. With this much income his personal allowance is completely withdrawn.

His salary and rental income take him up to the £150,000 additional-rate threshold. The first £5,000 of his dividend income is covered by the new dividend allowance, leaving £45,000 taxed at the 38.1% additional rate.

All of Martin's dividend income is taxable at the additional rate. The dividend allowance therefore reduces the amount of his dividend income taxed at the additional rate.

Chapter 6

More Tax Increases to Come?

Some tax experts fear that next year's dividend tax increase is just the start and further changes will be made to reduce the tax benefits of using a company and taking dividends over salary.

For example, the July 2015 Budget documentation states that: *"These changes will also start to reduce the incentive to incorporate and remunerate through dividends rather than through wages to reduce tax liabilities."*

Use of the word "start" may be a hint that further dividend tax increases, or other changes, are on the horizon.

In the July Budget the Government also announced that it will commission the Office of Tax Simplification to review the closer alignment of income tax and national insurance and to review the taxation of small companies.

The review of small company taxation will provide an initial report to the Chancellor before the 2016 Budget and will look at various issues, including:

- Whether and how tax affects the choice of business form and whether the choices faced by new and existing businesses can be simplified.

- Whether there are simpler ways that small incorporated businesses could be taxed, including the potential for a look through basis for taxing small incorporated businesses (i.e. taxing small company owners like sole traders and partnerships).

- The distortions between the personal and business tax systems.

It's impossible to predict what, if anything, will happen or when. However, it seems the Government is committed to removing "distortions" in the tax system which encourage people to do one thing instead of another purely on tax grounds, for example paying themselves dividends instead of salary or setting up a company instead of running their business as a sole trader or partnership.

Even after the new dividend tax rates come into force next year, most company owners will still be better off taking dividends rather than salary and many company owners will still pay less tax than unincorporated businesses (sole traders and partnerships).

So there is still scope for further tax increases in the future.

Chapter 7

Other Recent Tax Changes

Although the increase in dividend tax rates was bad news for company owners there were other tax announcements in the July 2015 Budget that will be welcomed by most company owners:

Corporation Tax

Most companies currently pay 20% corporation tax. In the July 2015 Budget it was announced that the corporation tax rate will be cut further as follows:

- From 1 April 2017   19%
- From 1 April 2020   18%

So a company making a profit of £100,000 will pay £2,000 less tax in a few years' time.

When you consider that the previous Labour Government originally planned to raise the rate paid by small companies to 22%, these tax cuts are something to celebrate, even if it will be several years before their full impact is felt.

National Insurance Employment Allowance

Since April 2014 most businesses have received an allowance of £2,000 per year to offset against their employer's national insurance bills. In other words, if your business would normally pay £10,000 employer's national insurance, it now pays £8,000.

This allowance is a welcome tax saving for most small companies that have employees. In the July 2015 Budget it was further announced that the employment allowance is to be increased from £2,000 to £3,000 from 2016/17.

However, from April 2016, the allowance will no longer be available to companies where a single director is the sole employee.

Income Tax Thresholds

The Government has also committed to raising the income tax personal allowance (currently £10,600) to at least £12,500 by 2020/21.

It has also committed to raising the higher-rate threshold to at least £50,000 by 2020/21.

As a result some company owners who are currently higher-rate taxpayers (paying 25% tax on some of their dividend income) may become basic-rate taxpayers and pay just 7.5% tax.

For example, a company owner who receives a cash dividend of £50,000 this year and has no other taxable income will pay tax of £2,963.

If they receive the same dividend in 2020/21 their tax bill will *fall* to £2,438.

Of course, this example is a bit simplistic because it ignores the effects of inflation (£50,000 in 2020 will probably be worth less than £50,000 today) and also assumes that there will be no further dividend tax increases in the meantime.

It also arguably illustrates a best case scenario – most company owners will still be paying more tax in the future than they do today.

Nevertheless, increases in the tax thresholds are likely to reduce the sting of the recent increase in dividend tax rates.

Chapter 8

Maximise Your Tax-free Dividends

At present if you're a basic-rate taxpayer you don't pay any tax on your dividend income.

On 6 April 2016 the era of tax-free dividends will come to an end and most company owners will start paying 7.5% tax on a big chunk of their income.

So the most obvious thing almost every company owner should do before 6 April 2016 is take the maximum amount of tax-free dividend income.

As it happens, this has always been the advice given to company owners, even before the increase in dividend tax rates was announced in the July 2015 Budget. However, it's more important than ever not to waste this year's tax-free dividend allotment because this is the last one you will get.

How much tax-free dividend income can you take? The answer depends on how much other taxable income you have.

For example, a company owner with no other taxable income can take a *gross* dividend of £42,385 which means he or she can take a tax-free *cash* dividend of £38,146 (£42,385 x 0.9).

A company owner with a small salary of £8,060 (the national insurance threshold for employees) can take a *gross* dividend of £34,325 (£42,385 - £8,060) which means taking a tax-free *cash* dividend of £30,892.

Similarly, a company owner with a small salary of £10,600 (equal to the income tax personal allowance) can take a *gross* dividend of £31,785 (£42,385 - £10,600) which means taking a tax-free *cash* dividend of £28,606.

Of course, many company owners take bigger salaries or have taxable income from other sources (e.g. rental income). In these cases the amount of tax-free dividend income that can be taken will be lower.

TABLE 2
Maximum Tax-free Dividends 2015/16

Taxable Income	Maximum Gross Dividend	Maximum Cash Dividend	Tax Saving
0	42,385	38,147	2,861
8,060	34,325	30,893	2,317
10,600	31,785	28,607	2,145
12,000	30,385	27,347	2,051
14,000	28,385	25,547	1,916
16,000	26,385	23,747	1,781
18,000	24,385	21,947	1,646
20,000	22,385	20,147	1,511
22,000	20,385	18,347	1,376
24,000	18,385	16,547	1,241
26,000	16,385	14,747	1,106
28,000	14,385	12,947	971
30,000	12,385	11,147	836
32,000	10,385	9,347	701
34,000	8,385	7,547	566
36,000	6,385	5,747	431
38,000	4,385	3,947	296
40,000	2,385	2,147	161
42,000	385	347	26
42,385	0	0	0

Table 2 shows the maximum amount of tax-free dividend income that can be taken in 2015/16, depending on the amount of other taxable income you will have for the year (including *gross* dividends already received).

For example, someone with a salary and rental income totalling £30,000 can take a tax-free cash dividend of £11,147. Someone with other income of £40,000 can take a tax-free cash dividend of just £2,147.

The 'Tax Saving' shown in the table represents the amount of tax saved by taking this additional dividend this year (when it is tax free) compared with taking it next year and suffering tax at 7.5%. This is discussed further below.

In some cases it may be difficult to predict how much income you will have from other sources and therefore how much tax-free dividend income you can extract from your company this year.

In these cases it may be necessary to err on the side of caution (i.e. pay yourself conservatively) or wait until closer to the end of the tax year when you may be able to estimate your other income more accurately.

If your other income turns out to be higher than expected this could push some of your dividend income over the higher-rate threshold, with 25% tax payable on the excess amount.

Example
Julian receives a salary of £1,000 per month from his company and has also paid himself a cash dividend of £10,000 so far this year (a gross dividend of £11,111).

He also owns rental properties. In the previous 2014/15 tax year he had taxable rental profits of £5,000. However, his profits were lower than normal because he spent around £10,000 replacing boilers. Looking at this year's property income and expenses he conservatively estimates that he will have taxable rental income no higher than £15,000.

As things stand his total taxable income in 2015/16 is likely to be £38,111 (£12,000 salary + £15,000 rental income + £11,111 dividend). This leaves him scope to pay himself an additional gross dividend of £4,274 (£42,385 - £38,111) which means he can pay himself a tax-free cash dividend of £3,847 (£4,274 x 0.9).

How Much Tax Will You Save?

Almost every company owner has nothing to lose by taking as much tax-free dividend income as they can this year. However, it's more difficult to calculate how much tax this will actually save you.

If you religiously extract the maximum amount of tax-free dividend income from your company each year, it may not be strictly correct to say that you are saving tax by doing the same thing this year. However, if you have not always extracted the maximum tax-free dividend each year, then it is fair to say that taking a bigger than normal dividend this year will save you tax.

Your tax saving will then generally be 7.5% of the additional dividend which you take this year.

For example, let's say you take an additional tax-free dividend of £20,000 this year. If this effectively replaces £20,000 of dividend income which you would have taken next year, or in some later year, and which would have been taxed at 7.5%, then it is fair to say that your tax saving is £1,500 (£20,000 x 7.5%).

Example
Nairn and Emme are married company owners. So far this year they've taken a salary of £10,000 each and a tax-free cash dividend of £9,000 each (a gross dividend of £10,000 each). They've taken roughly the same amount of income out of their company for several years now.

Following the dividend tax increase announced in the July Budget, they decide to declare the maximum tax-free dividend for 2015/16. With taxable income of £20,000 each they can declare an additional tax-free cash dividend of £20,147 each (see Table 2).

The company has sufficient distributable profits to cover these dividends, but Nairn and Emme do not wish to take the cash out of the company straight away, so their director's loan accounts are credited with the appropriate amounts: which can then be withdrawn tax free at any point in the future.

How much tax will they save? If we assume that both Nairn and Emme would otherwise have had at least £20,147 of additional dividend income taxed at 7.5% at some point in the future then their saving is:

£20,147 x 7.5% x 2 = £3,022

Table 2 contains more examples of how much tax you could save by taking the maximum tax-free dividend in 2015/16.

The next question is whether you should pay yourself even bigger dividends this year, i.e. should you pay 25% tax this year in order to save even more tax in the future?

Chapter 9

Should Basic-Rate Taxpayers Take a Bigger Dividend in 2015/16?

Let's say you've taken the maximum tax-free dividend from your company and now have taxable income of roughly £42,385 (the higher-rate threshold).

If you pay yourself any more dividend income this year you'll pay 25% tax. You may be happy to pay this extra tax if you need more money this year to pay your household expenses.

But is it worth taking a bigger than normal dividend this year simply to save tax, for example if you expect to become a higher-rate taxpayer in the future?

In other words, is it better to *definitely* pay 25% tax this year rather than *possibly* 32.5% next year or at some other point in the future?

Why would you expect to become a higher-rate taxpayer in the future? Perhaps you expect the profits of your business to grow significantly or you expect to receive more income from other sources, e.g. an inheritance.

Of course, you can only pay yourself a bigger dividend this year if your company has sufficient distributable profits (see Chapter 3). For the remainder of this chapter we will assume that it does.

Taking a bigger than normal dividend this year is arguably a high-risk strategy unless you are confident that you will definitely become a higher-rate taxpayer in the future.

If you are correct you'll save 7.5% (paying 25% tax this year rather than 32.5% in the future). But if you're wrong you will lose 17.5% (by paying 25% tax this year rather than 7.5% in future).

You might even lose 25% on the first £5,000 of any dividend if this would have been covered by the dividend allowance if it had been paid in the future.

Before you pay yourself a bigger dividend this year it's also important to remember that you'll be able to withdraw more dividend income from your company next year and possibly in future tax years before you become a higher-rate taxpayer and pay 32.5% tax.

Example

Solly owns Solly's Bottles Ltd, an online company selling wine from Uzbekistan. He always pays himself a tax-free salary equal to the national insurance threshold and the maximum tax-free dividend.

So far in 2015/16 he's taken a salary of £8,060 and the maximum tax-free cash dividend of £30,893 – total cash income £38,953.

The business is making good profits because Solly has discovered that many French consumers prefer Uzbek wine. This, along with the forthcoming dividend tax increase, convinces him to take an extra £10,000 dividend this year rather than next year.

The additional dividend results in an income tax bill of £2,500 in 2015/16 (£10,000 x 25%).

As it happens, Solly may be able to save tax by *postponing* the additional dividend until 2016/17. This is because, although dividend tax rates are going up, the higher-rate threshold for dividends will rise too (because they will no longer be grossed up).

If Solly waits until 2016/17 to take the extra dividend, quite a lot of it could end up being taxed at 7.5%, instead of 25% this year.

Example continued

In 2016/17, Solly takes the same basic salary and dividend of £38,953 that he did in 2015/16, plus an additional dividend of £10,000. He will then have total income of £48,953.

Solly will only pay 32.5% tax on £5,953 of his dividend income – the amount that exceeds the £43,000 higher-rate threshold. The other £4,047 of his additional dividend will be taxed at 7.5%.

Thus Solly will only pay £2,238 tax on the £10,000 additional dividend if he takes it in 2016/17, compared with £2,500 in 2015/16.

What this example shows is that a company owner whose current income is already equal to the higher rate threshold, and who intends, or expects, to keep their regular annual income at the same level in the future, would be better off deferring the first £4,047 of any additional 'one-off' dividend income until next year, so that it will be taxed at 7.5% instead of 25%.

Where someone like Solly wishes to take some additional 'one-off' income of more than £4,047, however, then they will be better off taking the **excess** as an additional dividend this year, as it will be taxed at 25% instead of 32.5%.

Following this approach for his additional £10,000 dividend would mean that Solly paid tax at 25% on an additional dividend of £5,953 taken in 2015/16, plus 7.5% on the additional sum of £4,047 taken in 2016/17.

This totals £1,792, which provides a saving of £708 compared with taking the whole £10,000 dividend in 2015/16, or £446 compared with taking the whole dividend in 2016/17.

Clearly, splitting any additional dividends in this way produces the best result.

The position would be different if the company owner expects to take at least £43,000 (the higher rate threshold for 2016/17) out of their company next year; and similar sums in future years.

In this case, the whole of any additional 'one-off' payment is generally better taken this year, as it will be taxed at 25% instead of 32.5%.

In other words, it is only when future dividend income is expected to be taxed at 32.5% (or more) that it will be worth taking additional dividend income in excess of the higher rate threshold this year and paying tax at 25%.

Maximising Tax Savings

Table 3 sets out the optimum position for company owners who have different amounts of income from other sources. For ease of illustration, 'Other Income' is assumed to be the same amount in both 2015/16 and 2016/17.

'Other Income' includes any salary taken out of the owner's own company, but does not include any earlier dividends already taken out of the company. It does, however, include the gross amount of any dividends from other sources (e.g. investments), as well as interest, rental income, pensions, etc.

Any earlier cash dividends already taken out of the owner's own company during 2015/16 will of course need to be included within the maximum tax-free dividend available for the year.

The optimum position is achieved by taking dividends in the following order of preference:

i)   The maximum tax-free dividend for 2015/16

ii)   Any dividends covered by the personal allowance in 2016/17 (£11,000)

iii)   Up to £5,000 of tax-free dividend for 2016/17 (i.e. the amount of dividend allowance available after deducting any dividends received from other sources)

iv)   The maximum amount of dividends for 2016/17 which are taxed at 7.5%

v)   Additional dividends taxed at 25% in 2015/16

In other words, it is only when the payments under (i) to (iv) have been exhausted that the company owner should consider taking additional dividends taxed at 25% in 2015/16.

The impact of any additional dividends taken in 2015/16 on the high income child benefit charge should also be taken into account.

TABLE 3
Optimum Dividends

Other income	Tax-free dividend 2015/16	Tax-free dividend 2016/17	Taxed at 7.5% 2016/17	Total for (i) to (iv)
0	38,147	16,000	27,000	81,147
8,060	30,893	7,940	27,000	65,833
10,600	28,607	5,400	27,000	61,007
12,000	27,347	5,000	26,000	58,347
14,000	25,547	5,000	24,000	54,547
16,000	23,747	5,000	22,000	50,747
18,000	21,947	5,000	20,000	46,947
20,000	20,147	5,000	18,000	43,147
22,000	18,347	5,000	16,000	39,347
24,000	16,547	5,000	14,000	35,547
26,000	14,747	5,000	12,000	31,747
28,000	12,947	5,000	10,000	27,947
30,000	11,147	5,000	8,000	24,147
32,000	9,347	5,000	6,000	20,347
34,000	7,547	5,000	4,000	16,547
36,000	5,747	5,000	2,000	12,747
38,000	3,947	5,000	0	8,947
40,000	2,147	5,000	0	7,147
42,000	347	5,000	0	5,347
42,385	0	5,000	0	5,000

Notes

1. "Tax-free dividend 2015/16" is the maximum tax-free cash dividend that can be taken in 2015/16, taking your income up to the £42,385 higher-rate threshold. This is item (i) above.

2. "Tax-free dividend 2016/17" is the maximum tax-free dividend that can be taken in 2016/17 by utilising your personal allowance (where available) and your £5,000 dividend allowance. Assumption: no dividends from other sources are received in 2016/17. This is the sum of items (ii) and (iii) above.

3. "Taxed @ 7.5% 2016/17" is the maximum amount of dividend falling into the basic rate band in 2016/17 and taxed at just 7.5%, This is item (iv) above.

4. "Total for (i) to (iv)" is total cash dividends that can be taken out in 2015/16 and 2016/17 combined which will either be tax free or taxed at just 7.5%. These are the total dividends which the owner should seek to take from their company before looking to take any additional dividends in 2015/16 which will be taxed at 25%.

For example, a company owner with existing 'Other Income' of £20,000 per year who wishes to extract a total of £50,000 out of their company during the period from 6 April 2015 to 5 April 2017 (the 2015/16 and 2016/17 tax years combined) should take the following cash dividends:

i) A tax-free cash dividend of £20,147 in 2015/16
ii) A tax-free dividend of £5,000 in 2016/17
iii) A further dividend of £18,000 in 2016/17 which will be taxed at 7.5%
iv) A further cash dividend of £6,853 in 2015/16 which will be taxed at 25%

Of course, what this actually means is paying a dividend of £27,000 in 2015/16 (£20,147 + £6,853) and a dividend of £23,000 in 2016/17 (£5,000 + £18,000).

Summary

Before you pay yourself a bigger dividend in 2015/16 and pay higher-rate tax at 25%, remember that you will be able to take more dividend income next year as a basic-rate taxpayer. This additional dividend income will be taxed at 7.5% but that's still better than paying 25% tax this year.

You may be able to make similar and possibly bigger additional dividend withdrawals in future tax years before 32.5% tax kicks in. This is because the Government has committed to raising the higher-rate threshold to at least £50,000 by 2020/21.

Remember also that, from 2016/17 onwards, your first £5,000 of dividend income each year will be tax free.

If you think your dividend income will exceed the higher-rate threshold next year or in a future tax year – despite the fact that your dividends will no longer be grossed up and despite Government promises to keep increasing the higher-rate threshold – then it may be worth paying yourself a bigger dividend this year.

You may wish to do this if your company has significant and growing distributable profits or you expect to receive more income from other sources which will push your dividend income over the higher-rate threshold.

Chapter 10

How Higher-Rate Taxpayers Can Save Tax

If you are *normally* a higher-rate taxpayer you may be able to save tax by paying yourself a bigger dividend this year (taxed at 25%) and possibly a smaller dividend next year or in a future year (taxed at 32.5%).

Example
Gabriella is a company owner who normally has a salary and rental income of £20,000 and cash dividend income of £40,000. With this much income Gabriella is always a higher-rate taxpayer, which means she currently pays 25% tax on some of her dividend income and next year will pay 32.5% on some of her dividend income. Her total income tax bill this year is £6,843 and will rise to £8,675 next year if she has the same income.

Because Gabriella is always a higher-rate taxpayer, she arguably has little to lose by paying herself an additional dividend this year in place of some of the dividend she would normally pay herself next year, or in some future year.

How much will she save? She'll pay 25% tax this year instead of 32.5% next year, a saving of 7.5% or £750 for every £10,000 of additional dividend income she takes.

How much additional dividend income can she or should she take this year? A key factor will be the level of the company's distributable profits – you can't pay yourself an additional dividend unless the company has sufficient distributable profits (Chapter 3). For the remainder of this chapter we'll assume it does.

Example continued
If Gabriella has the same £60,000 income next year (2016/17), £17,000 of her dividend income will be taxed at 32.5%. If she takes an additional dividend of £17,000 this year and reduces her dividends by £17,000 next year she will save herself £1,275 in tax (£17,000 x 7.5% saving).

If her company can afford it Gabriella could also consider paying herself an even larger dividend this year. For example, if she expects to once again have income of £60,000 in 2017/18, when the higher-rate threshold is £43,600, she will pay 32.5% tax on £16,400 of her dividend income.

So why not take an additional £16,400 now if she can and pay 25% tax instead of 32.5%? Gabriella may be able to do this but she has to be careful not to push herself into a higher tax bracket.

The £100,000 Threshold

Once your income exceeds £100,000 your personal allowance is gradually withdrawn. For every £2 of additional income you receive £1 of your personal allowance is withdrawn. Once your income reaches £121,200 in 2015/16 you will have no personal allowance left.

The practical implication for someone like Gabriella is she will pay tax at an effective rate of 48.6% on any additional dividend income she takes in the £100,000-£121,200 bracket – far more than she would normally expect to pay even after dividend tax rates increase next year.

Example continued

So far in the current tax year Gabriella has salary and rental income of £20,000, a cash dividend of £40,000 plus an additional cash dividend of £17,000. Her gross dividend income is therefore £63,333 (£57,000/0.9) and her total taxable income is therefore £83,333.

This means Gabriella can pay herself an additional gross dividend of £16,667 before her income breaches the £100,000 threshold and she starts to lose her personal allowance. This means she can pay herself an additional cash dividend of up to £15,000 in 2015/16 which will save her an additional £1,125 in tax (£15,000 x 7.5%).

However, she should not pay any further sums beyond this new cash dividend total of £72,000 (£40,000 + £17,000 + £15,000), as she would then start to lose her personal allowance and suffer an effective tax rate of 48.6%.

Although many higher-rate taxpayers may decide to pay themselves a bigger dividend this year (2015/16) and possibly reduce their dividends in future tax years, it's essential not to overdo it.

More specifically, it's essential that you do not deplete the company's distributable profits to such an extent that you cannot pay yourself a big enough dividend next year or in a future year to fully utilise your basic-rate band (where your dividends will be taxed at just 7.5%).

For example, if you take a big dividend this year and as a result your taxable income next year is less than the £43,000 higher-rate threshold, you will end up paying tax at 25% this year on income that should have been taxed at just 7.5% next year or in another future year.

Chapter 11

How to Protect Your Child Benefit

Child benefit is an extremely valuable *tax-free* handout from the Government. Parents who qualify currently receive:

Children	Total Child Benefit
1	£1,076
2	£1,789
3	£2,501
4	£3,214

plus 712.40 for each subsequent child.

Unfortunately, child benefit is gradually withdrawn where any member of a household has over £50,000 income. This is done by imposing a "high income child benefit charge" on the highest earner in the household.

Once the highest earner's income reaches £60,000, all of the child benefit will effectively have been taken away in higher tax charges.

For the highest earner in the household the child benefit charge creates the following marginal tax rates on dividend income in the £50,000-£60,000 tax bracket:

Children	Marginal Tax Rate on Cash Dividends
1	37%
2	45%
3	53%
4	61%

Plus 8% for each additional child.

The bottom line: If you want to pay yourself a bigger than normal dividend this year *and* your household receives child benefit, you may wish to keep your taxable income below £50,000 to avoid these extortionate tax rates. Why pay, say, 45% this year to avoid 32.5% next year?

The £50,000 threshold for Company Owners

If you've already taken a salary and the maximum tax-free dividend for 2015/16 your total taxable income will be £42,385. This means you can pay yourself an additional gross dividend of £7,615 before reaching the £50,000 threshold (£50,000 - £42,385).

This means the maximum cash dividend you can take is £6,854 (£7,615 x 0.9). You'll still pay 25% tax on the additional cash amount but will avoid the child benefit charge.

Income over £60,000

If your taxable income is normally over £60,000, one thing you may be able to do is pay yourself a bigger dividend this year and smaller dividend next year so that you avoid the child benefit charge next year and have less dividend income taxed at 32.5%.

Example
Craig is a company owner with taxable income of £70,000 in 2015/16 made up of a salary of £8,000 and gross dividend of £62,000 (£55,800 cash dividend). His wife Justine is a basic-rate taxpayer and receives child benefit of £2,501 for 3 children. If Craig has the same income this year and next year he'll pay tax of £8,714 in 2015/16 and £11,286 in 2016/17 – £20,000 in total. This includes high income child benefit charges of £2,501 in both years: the couple will effectively lose all their child benefit.

Craig therefore decides to pay himself an additional cash dividend of £15,000 this year and £15,000 less dividend next year. He'll pay tax at 25% this year on the additional dividend instead of 32.5% next year – a saving of £1,125.

Furthermore, because dividends will no longer be grossed up in 2016/17, Craig's taxable income for that year will be just £48,800: i.e. below the £50,000 child benefit charge threshold. Thus Craig will not have to pay the child benefit charge in 2016/17, saving the couple a further £2,501 (assuming child benefit rates remain the same for 2016/17).

This simple measure will thus save Craig a total of £3,626.

Chapter 12

High Income Earners

Income over £100,000

As mentioned in Chapter 10, once your income rises above £100,000 your personal allowance is gradually withdrawn. Once your income reaches £121,200 in 2015/16 your personal allowance is completely taken away.

As a result company owners with taxable income in the £100,000-£121,200 bracket face paying tax at a marginal rate of up to 48.6% on their cash dividends.

Many company owners with income close to the £100,000 threshold may therefore prefer not to pay themselves any additional dividend income in 2015/16, especially if the additional dividend will be relatively small.

Income over £121,200

If your taxable income in 2015/16 is already more than £121,200 (i.e. you have already lost your personal allowance) any additional dividends will be taxed at the regular rate applying to higher-rate taxpayers: 25% on cash dividends.

After that, the next threshold you have to watch out for is £150,000 where the additional rate of tax kicks in (30.6% on cash dividends). However, some taxpayers may be prepared to pay 30.6% this year rather than 32.5% next year.

Example

Eric is a company owner with taxable income of £140,000 in 2015/16 made up of a salary of £8,000 and gross dividend of £132,000 (£118,800 cash dividend). If Eric has the same income this year and next year he'll pay tax of £25,948 in 2015/16 and £33,835 in 2016/17 – £59,783 in total. In both tax years his personal allowance will be completely withdrawn.

Eric therefore decides to pay himself an additional cash dividend of £30,000 this year (a gross dividend of £33,333), even though most of it will be taxed at the additional rate (30.6%), and reduce his dividends by £30,000 next year. With total taxable income of £173,333 in 2015/16 his tax bill will be £34,615.

If next year he takes the same salary but reduces his cash dividends from £118,800 to £88,800 he'll have taxable income of just £96,800. Because his dividends will no longer be grossed up his income will be less than £100,000 and he'll hold onto all of his personal allowance. His total income tax bill will be £19,510. The combined tax bill for both years will then be £54,125.

Thus by taking a bigger dividend this year and smaller dividend next year his total income tax bill for both years falls by £5,658.

Income over £150,000

If your taxable income in 2015/16 is already more than £150,000 any additional cash dividends will be taxed at 30.6% compared with 38.1% next year.

However, because dividends will no longer be grossed up it will be possible to withdraw more income from your company next year before you become an additional-rate taxpayer.

Example

Gregory is a company owner with cash dividend income of £157,500 in 2015/16 (a gross dividend of £175,000). He has no other income. If he has the same income this year and next year he'll pay tax of £33,473 in 2015/16 and £43,233 in 2016/17 – £76,706 in total.

Gregory decides to pay himself an additional cash dividend of £25,000 this year (a gross dividend of £27,778) and reduce his dividends by £25,000 next year. With total taxable income of £202,778 in 2015/16 his tax bill will be £41,112.

If next year he reduces his cash dividends from £157,500 to £132,500 he won't have to pay the 38.1% additional rate and his total income tax bill will be £34,688. The combined tax bill for both years will then be £75,800.

Thus by taking a bigger dividend this year and smaller dividend next year his total income tax bill for both years falls by £906, which is not a very impressive tax saving for someone with so much income.

Why is the tax saving so small? Even if Gregory doesn't reduce his dividends in 2016/17, very little will be subject to additional rate tax anyway – just £7,500 compared with £25,000 this year. This is because his dividends will no longer be grossed up.

Chapter 13

Splitting Income with Your Spouse

Splitting company profits with a spouse or partner has always been a popular tax planning strategy and will probably continue to be so once dividend tax rates increase on 6 April 2016.

This strategy is typically used when both spouses are actively involved in the business but also when one of them is a "silent shareholder" with a lower tax rate than the person actively running the business.

However, there are traps to watch out for and such a strategy is not without risk (see the Taxcafe guide *Salary versus Dividends* for more details). For example, it is usually recommended that the 'silent shareholder' receives ordinary shares which give them full ownership and voting rights. Where the 'silent shareholder' is the spouse of the active shareholder/director it is also usually recommended that they receive an outright gift of shares in the company.

Tax savings typically arise where one spouse is a higher-rate taxpayer and gifts shares to their spouse who either has no other income or is a basic-rate taxpayer.

At present, the spouse who has no income or is a basic-rate taxpayer can receive tax-free dividends by following this strategy. Next year they could end up paying 7.5% tax but the first £5,000 will be tax free thanks to the new dividend allowance and a further £11,000 will be covered by their personal allowance if they don't have any other income.

Example

John owns 50% of Greasy Motors Ltd, a company that renovates classic cars. His wife Olivia owns the other 50% but is not actively involved in the business. The company makes after-tax profits of roughly £80,000 per year. John pays himself a tax-free salary of £8,000 (Olivia doesn't receive a salary because she doesn't work in the business) and the company pays both John and Olivia a dividend of £40,000 per year. The couple have no other income.

This year John will pay £2,263 in tax and Olivia will pay £463. The couple's total tax bill will be £2,726.

Next year (2016/17) if the couple receive the same income, John's tax bill will rise to £3,650 and Olivia will pay £1,800. The couple's total tax bill will be £5,450.

Although the couple's total tax bill will almost double next they are still better off splitting their income. If all of Olivia's dividend income was taxed in John's hands it would be taxed at 32.5% and the couple's total tax bill would be £16,650, an increase of £11,200!

By splitting their income in this fashion the couple benefit from Olivia's £11,000 personal allowance and £5,000 dividend allowance and the remaining £24,000 is taxed at just 7.5%.

Furthermore, because her dividends will no longer be grossed up, Olivia will be able to receive a further £3,000 of dividend income before she reaches the £43,000 higher-rate threshold (e.g. if the profits of the business increase).

Both Spouses are Higher-rate Taxpayers

Where both spouses are higher-rate taxpayers but one of them does not own any shares in the business, from 2016/17 it may be worthwhile for the spouse not actively involved in the business to have a small shareholding to utilise their £5,000 dividend allowance.

Example
Anne owns 100% of Tudor Cloth Ltd, a company that makes period costumes. She takes a small salary to use up her personal allowance (despite the small national insurance cost), leaving the company with after-tax profits of around £50,000 per year, most of which she withdraws each year as dividends. Her husband Henry has a job as a horse trainer and earns a salary of £60,000 per year. The couple do not have any other income.

Because they are both higher-rate taxpayers, Anne has never had any reason to gift shares in her company to Henry – he faces the same marginal tax rate as her.

However, because all taxpayers will be able to benefit from the new £5,000 dividend allowance in 2016/17, Anne decides to gift 10% of the company to Henry. This will enable him to receive a tax-free dividend of £5,000 per year. Because Anne would have paid 32.5% tax on this income this will save the couple £1,625 per year in tax (assuming there are no further dividend tax changes!)

Spouse Has Higher Tax Rate

Where the company owner is a basic-rate taxpayer but their spouse who is not involved in the business is a higher-rate taxpayer (or maybe an additional-rate taxpayer) it may also be worth gifting them some shares but the potential tax saving is much smaller – and riskier!

Example
Samson owns 100% of Samson Hair Ltd, a company that sells hair extensions. He takes a small salary to use up his personal allowance (despite the small national insurance cost) and the company is normally left with after-tax profits of £20,000 per year which he withdraws as a dividend. Up until now his dividends have been tax free. Starting in 2016/17 he'll pay 7.5% tax, although the first £5,000 will be tax free. His wife Delilah is a solicitor and earns a salary of £50,000 per year. The couple do not have any other income.

Samson decides to gift 25% of the business to Delilah to make full use of her £5,000 dividend allowance, potentially saving the couple £375 in tax (£5,000 x 7.5%).

This is potentially a high-risk strategy for such a modest saving because, if the profits of the business grow significantly, it is possible your spouse could end up paying 32.5% tax on a significant chunk of their dividend income.

Example continued
In 2016/17, Samson Hair Ltd's after-tax profit grows from £20,000 to £30,000. If Samson owns 100% of the shares he will pay just £1,875 income tax if he withdraws the money as a dividend taxed at 7.5%

(the first £5,000 will be tax free). If he owns 75% he will pay £1,313 income tax on his £22,500 dividend but Delilah will pay £813 tax on her £7,500 dividend. The first £5,000 of her dividend income will be tax free but the remaining £2,500 will be taxed at 32.5%. In total the couple will be £251 worse off.

When adopting this risky strategy, it is also important to remember that any dividend income received from other sources will use up part of the dividend allowance.

For example, if Delilah received dividends of £200 from investments in 2016/17, this would leave only £4,800 of her dividend allowance available. Only £4,800 of her dividends from Samson Hair Ltd would then be tax free, leaving her exposed to tax at 32.5% on £2,700 of her dividends. The couple would then be £316 worse off than they would have been if Samson had retained all of his shares in the company.

Summary

Couples may be able to save income tax in future by splitting their dividend income.

In some cases it is worthwhile for a spouse or partner who is not actively involved to receive shares in the business, even if they have income from other sources and are higher-rate taxpayers (although there are certain traps that have to be avoided so it is always wise to take professional advice).

However, when deciding whether to gift shares in your business to your spouse or partner it is important to look beyond the savings that may be made in a single year and not do anything you will regret if tax rules change or your financial position changes.

There are also non-tax reasons why transferring a portion of your business to your spouse or partner may be inadvisable: for example if you are unwilling to relinquish control of the company.

Note that, whilst a transfer of shares to your spouse or civil partner will usually be exempt from capital gains tax, a similar transfer to an unmarried partner may give rise to a capital gains tax liability in some circumstances.

Chapter 14

Pension Contributions

Company pension contributions may become more popular after dividend tax rates increase next year, especially with company owners who have reached the minimum pension age (currently 55).

Like salaries, company pension contributions provide corporation tax relief for the company. Furthermore, there is no immediate tax liability for the director.

Tax is payable when you start withdrawing money from your pension plan but 25% can be taken tax free and the rest can be withdrawn gradually so that, in many cases, tax at no more than 20% is payable.

Unlike dividends, pension contributions can be made without requiring accounts that show sufficient distributable profit.

Pension Contributions: You or the Company?

Company owners can choose between making pension contributions personally or getting their companies to make them.

Pension contributions you make personally cannot exceed your *earnings*, which means directors who pay themselves a small salary can only make a relatively small pension contribution each year (salaries count as earnings, dividends do not).

Company pension contributions are not restricted to earnings but, along with your own personal contributions, cannot exceed the annual allowance (currently £40,000).

Furthermore, there is a danger that HMRC will deny corporation tax relief for 'excessive' company pension contributions, for example if your total remuneration package (including salary, pension contributions and other benefits in kind) is excessive relative to the work you carry out and your company responsibilities.

When dividend tax rates increase on 6 April 2016, it seems that company pension contributions will become slightly more tax efficient than contributions made personally by the director.

Example

Cristina is a company owner with a salary of £11,000 and dividend income of £20,000 in 2016/17 (i.e. she is a basic-rate taxpayer). The company has a further £10,000 of pre-tax profits that she would like to use to fund a pension contribution.

She has two choices: get the company to make the contribution or take an additional dividend and make it personally.

If the company makes the contribution it can pay £10,000 directly into her pension plan, no corporation tax will be payable and there will be no income tax consequences for Cristina.

If she decides to make the contribution personally, the company will have to pay 20% corporation tax on the £10,000 profit, leaving £8,000 available to pay out as an additional dividend. When she pays this amount into her pension plan the taxman will add £2,000 of basic-rate tax relief, giving her an identical gross pension contribution of £10,000.

However, she'll still have to pay 7.5% income tax on the £8,000 additional dividend that she pays into her pension – a total of £600. Thus Cristina is £600 worse off making the pension contribution personally.

If Cristina was a higher-rate taxpayer she would still be worse off making the pension contribution personally but the penalty will be quite small thanks to the way higher-rate tax relief is calculated.

With a gross pension contribution of £10,000 her basic-rate band will be increased by £10,000, so an extra £10,000 of her dividend income will be taxed at 7.5% instead of 32.5%. So although she will pay 32.5% tax on the additional £8,000 dividend she takes to fund the pension contribution (£2,600) an additional £10,000 of her other dividend income will be taxed at 7.5% instead of 32.5% (a saving of £2,500).

In this case Cristina will be just £100 worse off making the contribution personally and may prefer to go down this route if she is nervous that her company pension contribution will be challenged by HMRC.

Pension Contribution or Dividend in 2015/16?

With dividend tax rates going up on 6 April 2016 some company owners with limited resources may face difficulty coupling any additional dividend withdrawals with pension contributions.

For example, if you pay yourself a bigger than normal dividend this year as a higher-rate taxpayer you may be able to avoid the 25% tax charge by making an offsetting pension contribution.

However, you may not be able to afford to lock the money away in a pension if you also intend to take a smaller than normal dividend next year – you'll need the money to pay the bills!

Other company owners may be toying with the idea of halting company pension contributions this year to free up resources to make bigger than normal dividend withdrawals, followed perhaps by bigger than normal company pension contributions next year.

It's a difficult juggling act and there are no easy answers. It doesn't help that the Government still seems to be toying with the idea of limiting tax relief on pension contributions.

There are no firm proposals as of yet but the Government has invited comments about making pensions more like ISAs, i.e. having pension contributions made out of *after-tax income* (with some sort of top up from the Government) and tax-free withdrawals when you retire.

Less radical changes could include retaining the current system and reducing the lifetime and annual allowances.

Because the future of pension tax relief remains uncertain some pension experts believe that it may be wise to make hay while the sun is still shining, i.e. to make pension contributions sooner rather than later.

Sample Documentation

1. Director's Board Meeting Minute

BOARD MINUTE

Minutes of a Meeting of Directors of Standard Ltd held at 100 London Road, Newtown, ZZ10 1AA on 31st March 2016.

Present:　　　Mr A B Crown – Director
　　　　　　　Mrs D E Crown – Director
　　　　　　　Mr E F Bloodaxe - Director

In attendance: Mr H Godwinson – Company Secretary

Motions:
　　1) It was recommended that the company pay a dividend of £2.50 per Ordinary share out of the profits for the year ended 31st December 2015, to be paid on 1st April 2016.
　　2) The directors noted the company's excellent trading results for the year ended 31st December 2015 with satisfaction.
　　3) No other motions.

Signed _____　　Date _____
　　　　　(Mr A B Crown)

Notes (Not Part of the Minute)
The minutes of a directors' board meeting should:
　　a) Indicate the persons present.
　　b) Include sufficient information to describe how directors reasonably came to reasonable decisions.
　　c) Include details of any conflicts of interest or abstainment from voting.
　　d) Be signed by a director present at the meeting.
　　e) Be retained with the company's statutory records.

Regarding point (a) above, a quorum may need to be present for the meeting to be valid. This depends on the company's own constitution as set out in its Articles of Association.

2. Member's General Meeting Minute

GENERAL MEETING OF MEMBERS

Minutes of an Extraordinary General Meeting of the Ordinary Shareholders of Standard Ltd held at 100 London Road, Newtown, ZZ10 1AA on 31st March 2016.

Present: Mr A B Crown – Ordinary shareholder
                 Mrs D E Crown – Ordinary Shareholder
                 Mr E F Bloodaxe – Ordinary Shareholder

In attendance: Mr H Godwinson – Company Secretary

Motions:
   1) The members, all being present, agreed to accept the short notice period for the meeting.
   2) The members approved the recommendation of the directors that the company pay a dividend of £2.50 per Ordinary share for the year ended 31st December 2015. Payment to be made on 1st April 2016.
   3) No other motions.

Signed _____   Date _____
          (Mr A B Crown)

3. Dividend Voucher

Tax Voucher

Standard Limited
100 London Road, Newtown, ZZ10 1AA

Ordinary shares of £1 each

Mr A B Crown   1st April 2016
1 Viking Crescent
York
Y1 1AA

Payment of the final dividend in respect of the year ended 31st December 2015, at the rate of £2.50 per share on the Ordinary Shares registered in your name on 31st March 2016 is enclosed herewith.

H. Godwinson, Company Secretary

Shareholding	Tax Credit	Dividend Payable	Payment Number
10,000	£2,777.78	£25,000.00	11

This voucher should be kept. It will be accepted by HM Revenue & Customs as evidence of a Tax Credit.